ANIMAL ARCHITECTS

BIRDS

by Karen Latchana Kenney

Ideas for Parents and Teachers

Pogo Books let children practice reading informational text while introducing them to nonfiction features such as headings, labels, sidebars, maps, and diagrams, as well as a table of contents, glossary, and index.

Carefully leveled text with a strong photo match offers early fluent readers the support they need to succeed.

Before Reading

• "Walk" through the book and point out the various nonfiction features. Ask the student what purpose each feature serves.

• Look at the glossary together. Read and discuss the words.

Read the Book

• Have the child read the book independently.

• Invite him or her to list questions that arise from reading.

After Reading

• Discuss the child's questions. Talk about how he or she might find answers to those questions.

• Prompt the child to think more. Ask: Have you ever seen a nest? Did you see the birds building it?

Pogo Books are published by Jump!
5357 Penn Avenue South
Minneapolis, MN 55419
www.jumplibrary.com

Library of Congress Cataloging-in-Publication Data

Names: Kenney, Karen Latchana, author.
Title: Birds / by Karen Latchana Kenney.
Description: Minneapolis, MN: Jump!, Inc., [2018]
Series: Animal architects | Audience: Ages 7-10.
Includes bibliographical references and index.
Identifiers: LCCN 2016051677 (print)
LCCN 2016054385 (ebook)
ISBN 9781620316948 (hardcover: alk. paper)
ISBN 9781624965715 (ebook)
Subjects: LCSH: Birds—Juvenile literature.
Birds—Habitations—Juvenile literature.
Classification: LCC QL676.2 .K46 2018 (print)
LCC QL676.2 (ebook) | DDC 598—dc23
LC record available at https://lccn.loc.gov/2016051677

Editor: Kirsten Chang
Book Designer: Michelle Sonnek
Photo Researcher: Michelle Sonnek

Photo Credits: Tobie Oosthuizen/Shutterstock, cover; Frank Greenaway/Getty, 1; IrinaK/Shutterstock, 3; Roman Pyshchyk/Shutterstock, 3; robertharding/SuperStock, 4; Anne Powell/Shutterstock, 5; Lovely Bird/Shutterstock, 6-7; Lorne Chapman/Alamy Stock Photo, 8-9; Joy Brown/Shutterstock, 10; Bruce MacQueen/Shutterstock, 11; FLPA/SuperStock, 12-13; Nico van Kappel/SuperStock, 14-15; John Cancalosi/Nature Picture Library, 16-17; dedek/Shutterstock, 18; muratart/Shutterstock, 18; Richardom/Alamy Stock Photo, 19; Paul Nicklen/Getty, 20-21; Ti Santi/Shutterstock, 23.

Printed in the United States of America at Corporate Graphics in North Mankato, Minnesota.

TABLE OF CONTENTS

CHAPTER 1
GRASS WEAVERS

A weaverbird finds two tree branches. They make an upside-down Y.

Its grass nest begins with a knot. Then the bird builds a strong ring. It winds grass up and down, in and out of the ring. Soon it will have a **dome** and a tunnel door, too. This woven nest keeps eggs safe inside.

beak

wings

feet

Birds are busy builders. All birds have body parts that help them build. Their hard beaks grab, push, and pull. Birds have wings, too. Most birds can use them to fly to find building materials. Their feet stomp and push inside a nest.

DID YOU KNOW?

There are more than 10,000 kinds of birds. The bee hummingbird is the smallest bird. It weighs less than a dime. The biggest bird is the ostrich. It's taller than a grown person.

All birds lay eggs with shells. Baby birds grow inside. Birds build nests to protect their eggs and keep them warm.

Birds use all kinds of building materials. They find moss, grass, spider webs, twigs, and more. Some even use their own feathers or bits of people's garbage.

CHAPTER 2

. . . .

BUILDING NESTS

Many bird nests start with twigs. A robin drops twigs in a **notch** on a tree. Its feet push the twigs to make a cup shape.

The bird adds smaller twigs with its beak. It uses mud as glue. Moss or grass makes the nest soft and warm inside.

Sticky spit helps birds make nests, too. A swiftlet makes its bowl-shaped nest mostly out of its own **saliva**. It hardens and sticks to cave walls.

A ruby-throated hummingbird also uses saliva. It makes a sticky disk out of its own saliva. It attaches the disk to a branch. Then the bird builds a cup-shaped nest on top of the disk. It uses spider silk, moss, and plants.

DID YOU KNOW?

Eagles use big sticks to make **platform** nests. The biggest found weighed 6,000 pounds (2.72 metric tons). That's more than a car weighs!

female ruby-throated
hummingbird

Some birds dig their nests in the ground. A puffin makes a **burrow** in rocks or on a cliff. It digs with its beak. Then it kicks the dirt out with its feet. It lays eggs on feathers and grass at the back of the tunnel.

Eggs need to keep warm to **hatch**. Most birds sit on their eggs. But a Malleefowl digs a pit in the ground. It uses its strong feet to kick **leaf litter** into a pile. The eggs go on top. Then the bird covers the pile with sand. As the leaves **decay**, they make heat for the eggs.

TAKE A LOOK!

A Malleefowl buries its eggs in a mound.
This keeps the eggs warm.

▪ = sand   ■ = eggs
▪ = leaf litter   ■ = Malleefowl
▪ = soil pit

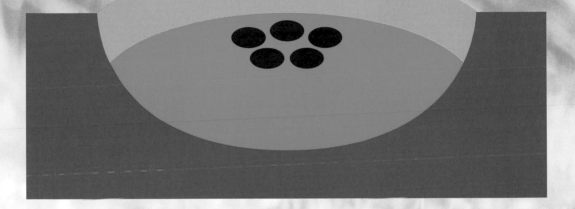

CHAPTER 3

BIRD NESTS IN NATURE

Bird nests can have both negative and positive effects on the environment. Birds can invade people's homes.

The sparrow sometimes makes its nest in a house's vents. It can stop **vents** from working. And baby sparrows can fall down pipes and get hurt.

vent

Birds can also help the environment as they build their nests. Birds flying from place to place scatter seeds, promoting plant growth. Bird droppings can provide nutrients for the soil, too.

Underground or up high, birds build amazing nests. They find different ways to keep their eggs safe.

ACTIVITIES & TOOLS

MAKE A CUP NEST

Try making a cup nest. What makes it strong?

What You Need:
- bendy twigs
- long grass
- dirt
- water
- bowl
- feathers

❶ Bend some twigs into a cup shape.

❷ Weave more twigs in to fill the empty spaces.

❸ Add grasses around the twig cup. Weave the grass in and out of the twigs.

❹ Now mix some dirt with water in the bowl to make mud. Pat it into the inside of the twig cup. Fill in any holes or cracks. Then let it dry.

❺ Add feathers around the inside of the nest. How does it feel?

❻ Test your nest. Put a few rocks inside, like eggs. Does it seem strong or weak? How could you design a different nest?

GLOSSARY

burrow: A hole in the ground where an animal can live.

decay: To rot or break down.

dome: A roof shaped like an upside-down bowl.

hatch: To break out of an egg.

leaf litter: Decomposing leaves and other debris forming a layer on top of soil.

notch: A V-shaped branch on a tree.

platform: A flat, raised structure.

saliva: A clear liquid in the mouth.

vents: Openings that let out smoke or fumes.

INDEX

TO LEARN MORE

Learning more is as easy as 1, 2, 3.

1) **Go to www.factsurfer.com**

2) **Enter "birdarchitects" into the search box.**

3) **Click the "Surf" button to see a list of websites.**

With factsurfer, finding more information is just a click away.